Grassroots leadership (7)

Recollections by

Michael Hall

ISLAND (78) PAMPHLETS

Published March 2006 by Island Publications
132 Serpentine Road, Newtownabbey, Co Antrim BT36 7JQ
© Michael Hall 2006
mikeohall@hotmail.com

http://cain.ulst.ac.uk/islandpublications/

ISBN 1 899510 70 2

Farset Community Think Tanks Project received funding from
The EU Special Support Programme for Peace and Reconciliation
administered through the **Northern Ireland Community Relations Council**

Printed by Regency Press, Belfast

Introduction

Towards the end of 2005, the Community Think Tanks Project facilitated a series of discussions involving working-class Protestant women in Belfast. An account of these discussions was to form the basis of the very last pamphlet to be produced under 'Peace II' funding. However, soon after the final draft was agreed I was informed that certain people – *not* the participants – were unhappy with some of the comments the women had made, and advised that publication should not take place – in case 'anyone receives a knock at their door'.

As the project has never risked jeopardising anyone's personal safety, I agreed to abandon the pamphlet. However, I told the leader of the women's group that the fact that, *eleven years* after the declaration of a Loyalist ceasefire, Protestant working-class people still had to fear a paramilitary knock on the door for expressing honest opinions should act as a 'wake-up' call to their community. The irony in this particular case was that what the women had been saying was not really all that controversial. Indeed, in the opinion of others who read the draft their views came over as balanced and humane, and I regretted not being at liberty to share these views with a wider audience.

As the Community Think Tanks Project had submitted an application for 'Peace II Extension' funding, my intention was to facilitate a substitute Think Tank in the event of this application being successful. However, to the surprise of many people at community level, the project was turned down for funding. This seemed especially unfortunate given that the problems highlighted by the women's pamphlet confirmed that the need for debate and dialogue – such as promoted and facilitated by the project for some time – was as great as ever.

Although I felt confident that the Think Tanks Project would resume its work once an alternative funding source could be secured, there still remained the problem that this particular pamphlet needed to be produced quickly to meet agreed commitments. And the only recourse open to me was to turn to what was closest to hand: my own recollections (or some of them). I hope that the reader accepts that it was this dilemma – and not any attempt at self-promotion on my part – which was my reason for falling back on such subject matter. I also apologise for the somewhat chaotic nature of these reminiscences; perhaps on some future occasion I can pen a more coherent presentation.

Michael Hall

Michael Hall

The eldest of five children, I was born in 1949 in Sandbrook Park in the Sydenham area of East Belfast, in the shadow of Harland and Wolff Shipyard. Although our parents imbued us with strong ethical and moral standards, these derived not from any religious belief but from a secular humanism. Despite having been born into the 'Protestant' working-class community, and with close relations being members of the Orange Order and B-Specials, I never recall hearing the word 'Protestant' mentioned in our house, even when the streets outside were festooned with bunting during the Twelfth of July celebrations. Indeed, the first time I was made aware of that label was when it was used by Catholic friends. My parents, happy to embrace different facets of their Northern Irish heritage, sent me and the older of my two sisters to Patricia Mulholland's School of Irish Dancing in North Belfast. During a lull in one particular class we happened to be chatting with some of our classmates and one of them – with no hint of malice, only curiosity – asked me: 'Are you a Protestant or a Catholic?' When I replied that I didn't know, he responded: 'Oh, you must be a Protestant then, for a Catholic would know.'

Not that we could keep religion at a distance entirely. We moved from East Belfast to live just off the lower Ormeau Road, where I attended a local Primary School. During one particular class the teacher told all the pupils to bring their family Bibles into school the following day, and I innocently replied that I wasn't sure if we had one. She was livid, appalled that any household should be without such an essential commodity, and straightway marched me to the corner of the room where she made me stand facing the wall. When my parents heard of this they were equally livid, my mother ready to storm round to the school and throttle the overzealous teacher, but my father decided that it was better just to acquiesce, as he felt any action on their part might only rebound on me.

Both sides of my family were proud of their working-class roots – embracing occupations from shop assistant and shipyard plater to master-stairbuilder. My grandfather, on my mother's side, was the shipyard poet Robert Atkinson, who had copious quantities of poems, short stories and articles published in *Ireland's Saturday Night*. (Unfortunately for my later attempts to gather together a collection of his poetry,[1] he had submitted his material under different pseudonyms in an effort to prevent the Labour Bureau – the 'brew' – from finding out that he was supplementing his 'dole' with the occasional meagre payment. Indeed, one day two dole snoopers, their suspicions aroused, went to question the owner of the

---

1 See Island Pamphlet No. 4, *Idle Hours: Belfast Working-Class Poetry*.

newspaper – who unceremoniously showed them the door.

Local history and politics were not much to the fore in our household discussions – what was happening on the world stage was deemed far more noteworthy. Nevertheless, aspects of a local connection would surface from time to time. For example, my grandmother, on my father's side, was a Gray, and she claimed to be able to trace her family lineage to prominent United Irish leader Betsy Gray. Certainly within our home library a torn and tattered 1899 edition of *Hearts of Down* held pride of place. Not to be outdone, my mother's sister married a Munroe, who claimed lineage to Henry Munro, leader of the United Irish forces in County Down. Whether these aspects of my family ancestry were real or simply the product of wishful thinking I was never sure. But the fact that my uncle was both an Orangeman and a member of the Masonic did nothing to lesson his pride in this aspect of his family heritage – such are the anomalies of Northern Irish political and cultural life.

Closeted from the world of Protestant sectarianism – which I was eventually to experience – my awareness of Northern Ireland's religious divide first surfaced through my participation in Irish dancing. Now, my dancing skills were nil – in Ulster-Scots parlance I was a bit of a *pachle* – but my sister was excellent and amassed a sizeable collection of medals from the numerous competitions in which she competed. During one particular *feis* she performed so well that expectations were high that she would be overall junior girl winner. Although she actually came second both she and my mother were delighted. However, soon afterwards some of the other parents approached my mother and one of them said: 'Mrs Hall, we believe your daughter should have been placed first. And – to our shame – we suspect that one of the reasons she didn't was that the organisers didn't want a Protestant name listed as junior girl winner in the *Irish News* tomorrow.'

My mother was taken aback, but believed – and still believes – that there was some other, more acceptable explanation. But it was an unsettling experience, and when it was followed by a more deeply personal incident some months later, it alerted me to the fact that sectarian attitudes in Northern Ireland were not the sole preserve of only side of our community.

• • •

(The nature of these recollections necessitates that I must skip now to the beginning of the Troubles and how that period impacted on my life. But in the intervening years I developed not only a deep interest in history and politics, but a passion for exploring the scenery of Ireland as well as its castles, abbeys, dolmens, court cairns, stone circles and a wealth of other antiquities.)

• • •

On 5 October 1968 a civil rights march in Londonderry was halted by police at Craigavon Bridge. Northern Ireland Civil Rights Association organisers urged the marchers to disperse, saying that their point had been made. After some pushing and shoving, placards were thrown at the police and the latter responded by charging at the marchers, hitting out indiscriminately with their batons. To make matters worse this was all done in full view of television cameras. The following day I was part of a sit-down protest in Linenhall Street, Belfast, organised by students from Queen's University. The protesters retreated to the university where the organisation known as the People's Democracy (PD) was formed. Many of PD's core members, such as myself, were not students (although I did enter Queen's a year later to do a degree in Social Studies and Politics.)

The unfolding local situation, particularly since the emergence of the Civil Rights movement, had caught many young people here by surprise. Our attention had been focused almost exclusively on events abroad, especially the tragic war in Vietnam and the worldwide student revolt, which revealed its revolutionary potential during the 'May events' in France 1968.

Although my upbringing had been enthused with socialist ideals, my own extensive readings, coupled with the daily evidence of authoritarian Communism in practice – particularly the invasion of Czechoslovakia and the crushing of all the hopes of 'socialism with a human face' which had been voiced during the 'Prague spring' – had left me highly antagonistic to all forms of state-sponsored Marxism, and even liberation movements if I suspected that they embraced any element of Leninist elitism. To me, Marxism/Leninism resembled another authoritarian religion, and a very dangerous and oppressive one.

No, what attracted me were the constructive ideals of anarchism: the belief that ordinary people could run their own lives without needing recourse to capitalists, commissars, politicians, clergymen and others.[2] There were a few others who felt likewise, and the first meeting of what would become the Belfast Anarchist Group (BAG) took place on 5 October 1968 in a small candlelit room above a restaurant in Upper Arthur Street in central Belfast. However, the meeting was poorly attended, as many prospective members had gone to Derry for the aforementioned Civil Rights march – an early foretaste of the competing contradictions which lay ahead. As events on the ground now began to unfold it was clear that dormant passions and aspirations – of a type totally alien to my own upbringing – were being unleashed within and between the two communities here, and within a short time I would find that neither Irish Nationalism nor Ulster Loyalism was sympathetic to libertarian socialist ideals.

• • •

That my understanding of Northern Irish society was severely deficient was dramatically revealed to me at the Burntollet ambush on 4 January 1969. On 1 January forty PD members set out from Belfast City Hall on a 4-day march to

---

2 This is not the place to begin to dispel whatever stereotypical notions the reader might hold about a philosophy which has been so pejoratively presented in the media. Suffice to say that the anarchism which I find appealing has nothing to do with either bomb-throwers or chaos, but is something highly creative and life-sustaining.

Derry. Loyalist 'counter-demonstrators' dogged the march's progress, and there were sporadic outbreaks of violence. I hadn't started out with the rest of the People's Democracy but had received a phone call from BAG member and PD spokesperson John McGuffin on the evening of the 3rd, asking me to bring the BAG's banner for the final day's march into Derry. The Ulsterbus on which I travelled actually had to make a detour to avoid the march, and, seeing it in the distance (close to Burntollet bridge), I asked the driver to let myself and two others off and we proceeded on foot. However, as we made our way along a narrow country road we realised, with some alarm, that our way was blocked by a large crowd of Protestants, some of whom now surrounded us. I dreaded their reaction if they should discover the banner hidden under my coat – the two poles I was carrying would be enough to arouse their curiosity. However, just then the march came into view and luckily – for us, that is – the entire crowd ran towards it, some of them picking up stones from piles already prepared in a nearby field.

We could also see a number of police vehicles stationed not far away and we hurriedly made our way towards them. When I next looked towards the march I was shocked to see it almost obscured under a barrage of stones. Then the ambushers made a direct assault, and, unable to resist its momentum, some of the marchers were forced off the road and chased across an adjoining field.

The police pushed us away from the main attack and as we stood there, horrified but transfixed, we gradually began to be joined by those who had escaped the initial force of the ambush. More and more stragglers arrived, many with blood streaming down their faces. Eventually the decision was made to resume the march to Derry, with the BAG banner to the forefront – the People's Democracy banner having been lost during the ambush. As we got closer to the city we were joined by hundreds of local people who had been alerted to the ambush and had come out to support us. A short time later, as we proceeded along Irish Street, we were again attacked. As I sustained a flurry of head punches and body kicks I attempted to defend myself with the banner pole before it was roughly snatched from my grip. Moments later I looked over my shoulder to see that the banner had been set on fire.

Once we arrived in Derry's Guildhall and had time to let our emotions and adrenaline levels subside, I found myself lost in deep reflection. It had all been a bit of a shock to me – not only the physical shock of the bodily assault but a psychological, even cultural, shock. The men who had attacked me had faces brimming with hatred, a hatred I just could not fathom. I began to wonder whether my secular upbringing had really prepared me for the reality of my own society. I was having to learn fast, to make up for lost time. And, for the first time, I experienced a deep unease about what I and others, both knowingly and unknowingly, had helped to unleash.

• • •

The PD did make an effort to show that it was equally critical of the set-up in the Republic of Ireland. As part of this effort a march was planned to Dublin for Easter 1969, with the marchers being bused through the North – to avoid any unwanted confrontations – and then walking from there. Although it was a bit of a non-event, one incident is worth recording. At one of our nightly halts prior to our arrival in Dublin, John McGuffin and the BAG members discussed the way the march was falling apart, the product of both internal dissension and weariness. In light of this, McGuffin made a proposal which was put to other marchers present in the room, not only the BAG members. It being Easter Sunday the following day his proposal was for a small group to proceed in advance to Dublin, and mingle with the crowds waiting for the traditional Easter commemoration parade[3] to pass. Then, just as ageing President de Valera would be taking the salute from outside the GPO, we would walk straight into the front of the parade and produce concealed placards attacking both the Northern and Southern states. We knew that for such an affront we could expect a severe beating by the Irish Army and the Garda – maybe not in front of the TV cameras, but soon enough afterwards.

Those gathered to hear McGuffin's proposal agreed in principle as long as he could get at least 20 marchers to support it. However, with most marchers by that stage exhausted and more concerned with finding somewhere comfortable to lay their sleeping bags, we just failed to reach that figure and the idea had to be abandoned. It was a missed opportunity many later regretted, especially when they saw what an anticlimax the whole event turned out to be, and the way waiting Republicans in Dublin tried to manipulate proceedings. Some southern Republicans even tried to get the PD members to march through Dublin in strict military lines, rather than sprawl across the road in their usual anarchic fashion. Needless to say, they were told where to put their request.

•   •   •

At Ballymurphy estate on the Springfield Road on the evening of 31 March 1970 a crowd of Catholic young people – some of whom were to proudly style themselves the 'Ballymurphy Young Hooligans' – attacked British Army soldiers standing between them and the adjoining Protestant housing estate of New Barnsley, despite efforts to defuse the situation by vigilantes and local Republicans. Inter-communal tensions had been building up since that morning, when a Junior Orange parade from New Barnsley had marched onto the Springfield Road on its way to a rally in Bangor, and upon its return the anticipated violence had erupted. The serious disturbances which occurred over the next two evenings were to become known as the 'Ballymurphy riots', and were seen by many as a significant point of escalation in the Troubles.

It so happened that at that time an Italian film crew, whose members belonged to a radical left-wing organisation, were in Belfast, and having made contact

---

3   The government in the South ceased holding this official parade in the mid-70s.

with PD asked to be taken to Ballymurphy on the second evening of the riots. I was among a small group of PD members who agreed to fulfil their request.

When we arrived at Ballymurphy estate the scene which greeted us resembled a large-scale re-enactment of a medieval battle scene. Different 'formations' were drawn up lengthwise along that part of the Springfield Road. Lining one side of the road was a crowd of Protestants, waving Union Jacks, who jeered and cat-called across at their Catholic adversaries. Next came a line of RUC officers, some facing the Protestants, others keeping a wary eye for what might be happening on the opposite side of the road, where an equally vociferous gathering of Ballymurphy's Catholic residents lined the pavement. Finally, between the RUC and the Catholic residents stood the British Army.

Apart from the jeering and catcalls being exchanged across the road, there were no other signs of trouble, so we proceeded to escort the Italians through the 'lines'. We got the impression that the Army and RUC personnel might have otherwise barred our progress, but the presence of the bulky cameras seemed to act as our passport. However, as the Italian film crew began to set up their equipment, the rest of us felt quite uncomfortable, for we were left in limbo in a sort of no-man's land.

A few minutes later a roar of anger erupted from the Protestant crowd. It had been occasioned by an event which occurred yards from where we were standing: a Catholic male had clambered up a lamppost and secured an Irish Tricolour as high as he could reach, before hurriedly descending and disappearing into the crowd. A group of soldiers was moving towards the scene, perhaps intending to remove the offending article, when loud bangs just above our heads – made by empty milk bottles smashing against nearby houses – made everyone in the vicinity duck to avoid a shower of glass splinters.

The 'Ballymurphy Young Hooligans' had obviously been making preparations during the day, for numerous crates of empty bottles had been stored in readiness. For their part, the British Army clearly intended to be firmer in their actions than on the previous night, and within minutes 'snatch squads' were preparing to pursue the teenagers into the interior of Ballymurphy estate. As the troops came under a renewed barrage of bottles and stones loud orders were barked and, to the astonishment of the RUC, the soldiers began to don gas masks. Within moments a cloud of CS gas descended upon us, and with our eyes smarting painfully we endeavoured to escape this new threat.

We looked around for the Italians but they were nowhere to be seen. Then a number of RUC officers, also suffering from the effects of the gas, began to usher us back through their lines.

'Lads, it'll be safer if you go this way. I don't know what those bastards are playing at – they never warned us they were going to use gas!'

The problem was that this 'safe way' took us directly towards the crowd of angry Protestants, a few of whom now ran over and began firing rapid questions at the four of us. Luckily one of our number possessed a fortuitous ability to replicate different accents. Utilising one such 'voice' he managed to convince the Protestants that we were foreign freelance journalists.

'But where's your cameras?'

'The rest of our crew got separated when the gas was fired. We need to get back into Ballymurphy to rejoin them.'

'What about interviewing *us*?'

'We'd certainly like to do that – once we can meet up with our camera crew.'

'Aye, right; you're a fuckin' liar – nobody's interested in us Prods.'

Despite the palpable sense of menace, no physical action was directed towards us. Apart from our 'foreign' comrade, who continued to chat away amiably, the rest of us maintained a careful silence. We made our way to Britton's Lane, which we knew would lead us back into Ballymurphy.

The Protestant crowd halted at the top of the lane, eyeing us suspiciously. From their comments it was obvious that not all were convinced of our journalistic status, and an overheard suggestion to 'Let's get the bastards!' almost made the four of us break into a sprint there and then. After we had proceeded a few dozen yards one of our party did indeed suggest running, as we were now far enough down the lane to reach safety should the Protestants decide to pursue us. However, it was decided not to do so, and we proceeded as casually as we could, afraid to look over our shoulders.

When we reached the far end of the lane to our great alarm two men with guns suddenly stepped into our path. We walked up to them and their wary faces only relaxed when explanations were given and accepted.

The sequel to this story occurred some months later when one of our group present that night happened to be jailed on a false charge of rioting and by chance mentioned the incident to some Republican inmates. To his astonishment one of them burst out laughing, explaining that he and four others had been on armed guard that night and when they saw the crowd of Protestants standing at the top of Britton's Lane they assumed that a flanking attack on Ballymurphy was imminent. However, they couldn't understand why our small group had broken off from the main crowd, and debated how to respond. They decided that as long as we kept walking they would hold their fire, but if we started to run then they would open up!

During the Italian film crew's stay in Belfast, some of us had endeavoured to give them what we felt was a balanced picture of what was happening in Northern Ireland, especially important as the perceptions held by many outsiders were often abysmally inaccurate. (I once accompanied a carload of foreign visitors through the lower Shankill area, and was surprised when one of them asked me: 'Why do these Catholics paint their kerbstones red, white and blue?' 'This is a Protestant area,' I responded. To which they retorted: 'But how can it be – these people are poor!')

Although the PD was distrusted by most working-class Protestants, the latter could not have found much fault with the sympathetic picture we presented to the Italians of their community, lamenting the artificial divisions which had been created between the two sections of the working class. Naively, we had assumed that the Italians' left-wing credentials would mean that they would be receptive to our analysis. However, when we later saw the completed film we realised that our input had been a total waste of time, for not only was it a glorification of nationalism, but it had a very anti-Protestant bias. That Protestant who had confronted us at New Barnsley had been quite accurate in his assessment.

(This was not the only time I was to feel betrayed by the workings of the media, both international and local, for my disenchantment was to be reinforced over subsequent years through various encounters with journalists and documentary-makers. Not only have many media individuals proven themselves to be primarily interested in the violent and the controversial but they sometimes placed people's lives at great risk. Indeed, when one TV programme did just that, I endeavoured to interest other community activists in the idea of organising a community-wide media boycott. The idea never came to fruition, but in the course of those efforts Father Des Wilson wrote to me: 'We don't need them, because we don't need misinterpretation. Better for us to explain what we are doing to a hundred people than have it misrepresented to a million.')

· · ·

From its inception, many members of the BAG increasingly found their energies preoccupied with PD activities, and by 1971 meetings were sporadic and attended by only a handful. The end came in early 1973 after about half a dozen of us had met to discuss our disillusionment with the prevailing situation, not only the senseless blood-letting but the total absence of any cross-community socialist politics. The meeting also discussed recent allegations by the police in London that the Provisional IRA were being aided by local anarchists. It was agreed that I would issue a statement to the press refuting the claims, stating that as anarchists we refused to support any group which we felt hadn't the interests of ordinary people at heart, but instead kept itself in existence through authoritarian means and nationalist ideology (whether Irish nationalism or Ulster nationalism).

One BAG founding member, who had become a prominent figure within PD politics, was furious with the statement. To my astonishment he said that we should not have been criticising the Provos because 'they were the only ones killing British soldiers.' I was aghast. 'How can anyone professing libertarian socialist ideals come out with such an analysis?' I asked him. But he wasn't the only one. The Provisionals' 'armed struggle' – wedded to a purely nationalist agenda – seemed to be sucking many radical individuals along in its wake, and the purely internationalist and socialist ideals we all once shared seemed to be crumbling in the process.

(Another BAG founder member went even further. In the 1980s I was involved in organising children's holidays to Holland, and on one particular occasion happened to be showing Dutch visitors around West Belfast. While in Beechmount they noticed the Sinn Féin advice centre and asked me to take them inside, where I was surprised to find a former comrade manning the desk. When I got over my astonishment that he had joined Sinn Féin I asked him what economic structure Sinn Féin envisaged in their United Ireland: would it be capitalist, or a mixed economy, and was there any talk of workers' control?' His answer stunned me: 'We'll worry about all that when the Brits are kicked out!')

• • •

When the BAG folded, a handful of us formed the Belfast Libertarian Group, and, dismayed by the relentless violence and the rampant sectarianism, made what small contribution we could to counter this appalling situation. To begin with, we produced what we hoped would be the first in a series of documents which attempted to analyse the events unfolding around us. In a pamphlet *Ireland, Dead or Alive?* we not only castigated Unionist discrimination but the Provisional IRA's murderous bombing campaign. Reaction was almost immediate.

A close friend who had contacts with the Provisionals was given a 'message' from them to pass on to me: 'Tell your mate that if he writes anything like that again he'll get his knees ventilated.' Soon afterwards I was confronted by a group of Loyalists in Sandy Row whose warning was no less blunt: 'We're watching you, you bastard, and we're going to get you soon!'

Alongside the doomed pamphlet venture, we also produced a series of silk-screened posters, incorporating a numbered 'Know Your Enemy' theme in the hope that this might stimulate public interest. Our targets included sectarianism and working-class exploitation. We began to paste up these posters around North and West Belfast, but found it exhausting work for such a small group. When a member of the Official wing of the Republican movement approached us, saying how much he liked the posters and suggesting that his 'crowd' put them up in Catholic areas, we reluctantly let him become involved. And so his associates began to put up our posters by the hundreds.

When our contact first began to take posters we hadn't at that stage produced poster No. 5, focusing on the Churches, and when he saw it he looked quite alarmed and asked us not to do anything with it until he got back to us. He returned the next day, looking extremely worried: 'I've been told to tell you that we can't put that poster up. We've been seen putting all the others up, so people will assume they originated with us. And we can't be associated with any attack on the churches.' Somewhat ominously, he added that he had been instructed to warn us that *we* were 'not going to be allowed' to put up any either.

We put up two dozen of the offending posters in a gesture of defiance, then destroyed our entire stock. With hindsight, it was probably an ill-conceived move on our part to attack the churches so openly, but at that time we felt so angry at *every* sector in society – the Republican movement, the Loyalist paramilitaries, the Unionist establishment, the British government, the churches, the business community – for the terrible situation now confronting ordinary people that we fervently desired to lambast them all.

Shortly afterwards, while socalising one Saturday afternoon in Kelly's Cellars – a favourite PD haunt – I complained about all these impediments to what we were trying to do, and to my surprise was told by PD members present that it was all our own fault. They felt that we were totally naive, that any notion of promoting cross-community radicalism at that time was a total waste of time, as the two extremes had the situation sewn up between them and nobody else could expect to get a look in. This sober assessment was a final confirmation to me that the idealistic dream was over and the nightmare well and truly begun.

• • •

The threats received over the pamphlet and poster efforts – minuscule though they were in comparison to the tragedy which was engulfing so many lives all around us – were nevertheless enough to encourage my partner, Sheila, and I to get offside for a while. Within days of our marriage in the summer of 1974 we set off to Amsterdam to look for work. We were lucky to find employment, for Amsterdam then was a thriving Mecca for young people from all over Europe and any job vacancies were greedily snapped up. When we arrived there the 'youth scene' was so all-pervasive the city authorities had permitted a youth committee to establish 'sleep-ins' – cheap, hostel-type accommodation – and run a comprehensive youth support network. By day the city's multinational youth population congregated around the National Monument in Dam Square, observing and being observed, while at night they got high in music clubs like the *Paradiso* where soft drugs were openly available.

Amsterdam's central park – the Vondelpark – had also been appropriated. By day it was filled to capacity with young people, lounging in small groups or gathered in circles around any budding musicians. Crowds were liveliest around those music-makers who beat out a driving rhythm on drums and tom-toms, usually to the accompaniment of hypnotic chanting from enthusiastic spectators. By night the park became one vast dormitory, with sleeping-bags and plastic sheeting indicating the whereabouts of those who, like ourselves, had been unable to find room in the sleep-ins, or who just wanted to sleep rough for the experience. A main road crossed over a section of the park and in the walkway underneath an area had been sealed off for use as a depository for backpacks.

We spent three weeks trudging the docks, the markets, the industrial estates, in a vain search for work. We made daily checks with the staff at various work bureaux, hoping that familiarity might result in job offers. Then, just as our finances began to run so low that we contemplated moving to Germany, we both struck lucky, with a temporary job in a pickle-bottling plant for me and a position for Sheila in the foreign section of a Dutch bank. To any early morning strollers in the Vondelpark it must have seemed quite incongruous to hear an alarm clock go off amid the sleeping bodies sprawled upon the grass, then watch as two figures hurriedly arose, rolled up their sleeping-bags, deposited them in the 'luggage office' before rushing off to the nearest exit. It was a difficult routine which luckily only lasted a few days, for one of Sheila's work colleagues lent us her apartment while she went on holiday and then other Dutch friends found us a houseboat to rent.

The Dutch felt that these were all terrible hassles to have to contend with, but to us they were not hassles at all. The Belfast we had left behind was a place of nightmares. To compound the brutality of the IRA's 'armed struggle', Loyalist gunmen were conducting a barbaric campaign of indiscriminate assassinations, mainly directed at innocent Catholics but engulfing anyone who just happened to be in the wrong place at the wrong time. 1974 was particularly horrific, and there were periods when there was a new victim almost every night, and rumours of torture and mutilation had many people in a barely-contained state of panic. We had lived in a flat in Fitzroy Avenue off the lower Ormeau Road – sandwiched between what were perceived to be Catholic and Protestant areas – and in the evenings, if I had occasion to visit our local 'corner shop', I would hold my breath if I heard a car approaching, listening for the slightest indication that the vehicle might be slowing down, and when it was well past I would then release my breath in one long, tension-filled sigh.

We never realised just how insidious the whole process had been until, about a month after arriving in Amsterdam, one of Sheila's work colleagues commented:

'We were talking about you the other day, and we agreed that when you first came you looked constantly tense, wary. But that has slowly gone and you look far more relaxed now.'

It was only then that we understood just how deeply it had affected us. But gradually we reclaimed the freedom which had been stolen from us. Sometimes, in the early hours of the morning, we would leave our houseboat to go window-shopping along the deserted Kalverstraat, Amsterdam's main pedestrians-only shopping street. Our Dutch friends had been horrified to learn of this, for to them the Kalverstraat at that time of the day was considered dangerous territory, the haunt of petty criminals and drug addicts. But to us it only mattered that it was not Belfast, and that was enough.

• • •

After living a year in Amsterdam, we decided that we wanted to travel much further afield. In the mid-1970s the talk among adventurous young people in Amsterdam was of taking a 'Magic Bus' all the way to Goa or Kathmandu. Although the idea of sitting in a cramped bus did not appeal to us, such destinations certainly did. And so we returned to Belfast and made our plans. (The return journey from the Hook of Holland to Harwich was enlivened when, at the railway station at Harwich docks, English police officers came running along the platform, boarded both ends of our train carriage, ordered us off and detained us for several hours under the Prevention of Terrorism Act.)

Although our decision to embark upon an extensive overland journey was prompted partly by the realisation that there was little contribution we could make to grassroots politics at that time – and, in the wake of the previous threats, certainly not one without personal risk – such a trip was something I had long been contemplating even before the Troubles erupted. A good proportion of the second-hand books I had amassed over the years were devoted to travel and adventuring. And although these readings may have fuelled my appetite for long-haul travel in a manner absent from Sheila's experience, her willingness to embark upon our venture was just as evident. This was epitomised by her reaction when I showed her the route I proposed we take to India and back.

She scrutinized the world map spread before us for some moments, lost in thought. She had never expressed any hesitation up to now and her silence perturbed me.

'Are you happy enough with that?' I asked her, somewhat anxiously.

She leaned over the map and stretched her thumb and little finger to touch both Ireland and India, then moved her hand sideways so that her thumb and finger, still held the same distance apart, now touched India and Australia. She looked up, a clear determination etched upon her features.

'There hardly seems any point retracing all our steps from India when the same distance will take us to Australia?'

I smiled and watched as she continued to peruse the map, suspecting what was coming next.

'And, furthermore, there hardly seems any point in retracing our steps from Australia when we can just continue on round.'

Quite logical, really, when you think about it.

This is not an appropriate place to describe our next two years of travelling, which provided us with a host of unforgettable memories: being detained by the Turkish army and accused of spying for Greece; bumping across the desert-like landscape of northern Afghanistan in open-topped local transport; feeling not only sick but anxious as rickety old buses crawled their way around precarious hairpin bends high into Kashmir; trekking to the Annapurna Sanctuary in Nepal; smuggling spices from Sri Lanka into India; sleeping on the deck of an old riverboat plying the Irrawaddy River in Burma; living with local families in Indonesia, Malaysia, Fiji, New Caledonia and so many other places; working to replenish our finances in Australia; hitchhiking around Japan in the snow; travelling the length of the Trans-Siberian Railway in the middle of the Russian winter... and many other such experiences.

But one thing *is* worth recording here: the warmth and generosity we encountered in every country on our route only served to reinforce our already firmly-held belief that ordinary people's needs were the same the world over, as was their desire to see a better world for their children – *irrespective* of all the many and varied religious and cultural 'differences' which attempted to divide them.

•   •   •

When we returned to Belfast I went back to Queen's University to do a Master in Social Work degree, and on qualifying joined the NSPCC (National Society for the Prevention of Cruelty to Children). At that time NSPCC was undergoing a period of self-examination. Its centenary was approaching and it was attempting to redefine itself, especially in relation to its 'big brother', the Social Services. In such periods of questioning all options can seem equally viable, and I was permitted to develop my own 'community-orientated approach to social work'. I built up close links with numerous community groups in Belfast and Newtownabbey, operating an informal 'surgery' for some of them at selected times each week. These groups benefited from being able to provide an on-site social worker as part of their community outreach, and the close working relationships I developed with the groups helped to dispel some of the antagonism with which social workers had hitherto been viewed. On visits to the different community venues – if my time wasn't taken up with seeing 'clients' – I would often sit down with the community volunteers and explore how *they themselves* could best tackle the numerous problems they encountered.

I soon discovered ample evidence for what I had long believed – that within each community there existed an untapped mine of strengths and abilities. Time and again I encountered individuals – from young people to senior citizens – whose commitment, energy, understanding, and ability to empathise often exceeded that possessed by many trained professionals. All that these community volunteers required was a little guidance and support – yet all they too often received was avoidance and professional aloofness.

For example, in one estate a number of young women – all single-parents – had formed a group for mutual support, and they told me that because I had helped some of them with various problems they in turn wanted to help some of the families I visited. I explained that for reasons of confidentiality I could not reveal to them which families were on my caseload. However, I asked them, surely they already knew families with *similar* problems – what was to stop them from offering assistance to those families?

We explored just what *was* indeed stopping them, and it became clear that they were wary of what they might encounter, and anxious that they would not know how to handle it. What would they do, for example, if someone admitted to harbouring fears of injuring their child, or suddenly displayed deep-seated emotions? At least by getting involved in *my* cases, they could leave such problems to me. More earnest discussion followed, at the end of which we worked out the following agreement: they would identify suitable families to whom they would offer assistance, and, if accepted, would engage those families on the understanding that should they need advice I could be readily contacted. Should real problems surface they would suggest to the family that I become involved directly. It was also understood that if there was any suspicion of child abuse I would *have* to investigate, whether the family agreed or not.

In the event, those young women rarely needed to contact me, and in subsequent progress meetings I was surprised not only by the range of problems they had begun to tackle, but by the natural abilities they had been able to utilise. And all it had taken was the reassurance that professional assistance was at hand should problems arise – this had been the catalyst which permitted these natural abilities to flower.

As I repeated this approach with other groups, it was made known to me that other professionals (though not from within my own agency) were observing all this with disapproval. I was informed I was taking a risk entrusting serious matters to 'non-professionals'; I was demeaning my years of university training by imagining that social work skills could be imparted to community volunteers in half-hour 'chat sessions'; I was consorting with well-known community activists whose strident pronouncements against the prevailing social and economic conditions could cause my employers embarrassment; my presence was adding credibility to groups who might have overt political agendas; I was allowing community groups to dictate my workload....

It did not seem to matter to these critics that these community volunteers were well aware of what constituted a 'serious' matter, and were actually more willing than they had previously been to request professional assistance, because it now seemed less threatening and more supportive. It did not seem to matter that groups who genuinely cared about people's needs were inevitably developing a realistic appreciation of political and economic realities, and were prepared to challenge social inequalities, unlike many professionals. Or that these community groups actually helped me devote *more* attention to the work I was trained for, because while the groups referred the more difficult cases to me they in turn accepted *from* me all those tasks which had previously taken up an inordinate amount of my time – queries on social benefit, housing, debt and other such matters. No, what really seemed to be at the root of this professional antagonism was that there was a danger of revealing that social work skills were not something magical known only to the initiated, but were a combination of common sense reasoning and natural ability given direction by proper training. One professional actually complained to me: 'These young people could end up imagining they could do our job better than us.' What a shock that would be.

(After seven years with the NSPCC, I was eventually asked to relinquish the community-oriented approach to social work I had been building,[4] and, unwilling to do so, resigned and signed on the 'dole'.)

•　　•　　•

During my time as a social worker I was also engaged in various community-based activities. For a short period I was involved with community drama,[5] and Sheila and I were founder parents of Hazelwood Integrated Primary and College (where we sent our two children). Then I became voluntary co-ordinator of

---

4　For more on this period see Pamphlet No 14, *Reinforcing Powerlessness.*
5　See Pamphlet No. 5, *Expecting the Future.*

Kinder Community House, a cross-community residential facility located in Killough, Co. Down, funded by the Dutch children's charity Pax Christi Kinderhulp.[6]

Over the next few years I came into contact with, and had the privilege to work closely alongside, numerous community activists: people like Joe Camplisson, Louis West, Des Wilson, Jim McCorry, Noelle Ryan, Jackie Hewitt, June Campion, Jackie Redpath, Frank Cahill, May Blood, May Robinson, Joyce McCartan and Eilish Reilly (and, more recently, individuals like Róisín McGlone, Anne Gallagher, Tommy Holland and others).

But most of my contacts were with community activists, not with the paramilitary groups. Yet I felt, as did many other community activists, that we had to engage with such people. I particularly wanted to renew my cross-community efforts of the 70s, but was that safe? For example, the activities and murders of the largest Loyalist paramilitary organisation, the UDA, horrified me, and I could discern no redeeming features whatsoever about that organisation and generally dismissed its members as thugs and bigots. And then, in 1984, I came across a small book of poetry, *Concrete Whirlpools of the Mind*, written by Sammy Duddy, Public Relations Officer for the organisation. I was quite surprised, and greatly heartened, by the content of some of the poems, for they spoke of the fratricidal tragedy which was now engulfing Northern Ireland and of the manipulation of working-class Protestants by their own politicians. This put a totally new perspective on things, and I realised that I had forgotten my own rule of thumb: nothing is ever as it seems, and all organisations contain both the good and the bad. I resolved, therefore, to pay a visit to UDA headquarters in Gawn Street in East Belfast.

As I made my way across town I reflected that although I had been born in East Belfast – and my mother had been born in Ravenscroft Avenue, my father in Dee Street – it had become alien territory to me, both geographically and politically.

Andy Tyrie (then the UDA's Supreme Commander) was in the building and was able to see me right away. (I assumed this was just good fortune but I soon discovered that Tyrie was someone who always made time for visitors.) When I entered his office he welcomed me:

'Well, what can I do for you?'

I felt I had better just come to the point.

'Andy, I am an NSPCC social worker and all I am interested in is our children's future – *all* our children. And as far as I am concerned you people, the Republicans, and the security forces are making a bloody mess of this place.'

'Indeed?' he replied. He pointed to the massive table which adjoined his equally large desk and smiled: 'Then you better sit down and we'll have a talk.'

Before the conversation proceeded too far I said: 'I should also point out that, twenty minutes after leaving this building I will be visiting my good friend

---

6   See Pamphlet No 59, *'Home and Away'* for some recollections on the Dutch holiday scheme.

Father Des Wilson in Ballymurphy.'

'Well, give him my regards when you see him. Tell him I'd love to go for a walk up the mountain with him if we can ever achieve peace. I used to live in Ballymurphy, you know; we might have our differences, but the people there are good people.'

The meeting lasted over four hours, and was to be the first of many I would have over the coming years with Loyalist leaders – individuals like Joe English, Sammy Duddy, Gusty Spence and Billy Hutchinson – as well as those from a Republican background, such as Tommy Gorman, Jim McCorry and others.

• • •

I have numerous anecdotes relating to cross-community efforts in the 1980s and 1990s – involving my Loyalist and Republican contacts – which limitations of space requires me to leave to another time. But if I stick with the UDA connection for the moment, it might give some flavour of the contradictions which exist at all levels of our tragically divided society.

For example, at one stage I was involved (in collaboration with Dr Ian Adamson) in promoting the shared history of the people of Northern Ireland, and of the people of our two islands. (The intense debate the history issue engendered is covered elsewhere.[7]) As part of my efforts to stimulate cross-community awareness of our common historical and cultural inheritance I began work on a book *Ulster: the Hidden History.*[8] When I had the first draft completed I gave copies to various people in both communities, including Andy Tyrie and John McMichael of the UDA, and Martin McGuinness and Joe Austin of Sinn Féin. I wanted to see what they thought about the book's basic theme, and whether they felt any aspects of it could be improved or clarified. I was in Tyrie's office one day when McMichael came in and joined our conversation. Andy, with that mischievous look which indicated that he was 'mixing it', said:

'John, did you know that Michael was in Derry the other day talking to Martin McGuinness?'

At the mention of that name John expressed a few derogatory comments, clearly wanting to know whether I agreed with their tone and content. Tyrie laughed.

'John, you're wasting your time – Mike never runs anyone down. He'll not run them down in front of us, just as I have no doubt that he doesn't run us down in front of them.'

John smiled and then asked me:

'Okay, then: tell me this – what is McGuinness like as a person?'

The question stunned me, for it was a straight case of *déja vu.*

'John, I'll tell you why your question has surprised me. When I was with McGuinness, do you know what he said to me: "I know you are in contact with

---

7   See pamphlet No 7, *The Cruthin Controversy.*
8   Published in 1986 by Pretani Press, Belfast. A revised second edition was published in 1989.

the UDA, and I want to ask you something. We [Republicans] know the way we are demonised by the media, so when we see UDA leaders on TV we must assume that they are being demonised likewise. So tell me: what are Andy Tyrie and John McMichael like as people?" '

• • •

During my discussions at Gawn Street, I would also argue about the material which was appearing in the UDA's magazine *Ulster*, not only because I found much of it highly sectarian, but dangerous to those involved in community activism. For example, articles would frequently attack Father Wilson. I told both Tyrie and McMichael that whatever they thought of Father Wilson's politics he had far more concern for working-class Protestants than their own Unionist 'fur-coat' brigade. Tyrie agreed with this and, to his credit, stopped any further such attacks appearing in the magazine.

Another anecdote is equally illuminating. At that time the editor of *Ulster* was Jim Donaghy, and he got to know me well because of my constant urging to cut out the magazine's blatant sectarianism and encourage more progressive material. Then Jim informed me that he and his wife were going on their first holiday abroad for many years. (In retrospect it was as if Jim had an intuition that all was not well with his health, for a few months after their return he was to die of a heart attack.) I asked whether he was going on a direct flight from Belfast, and when he said that he was, I responded:

'Jim, when you're in your hotel I bet you that your best friends there will not be any other UK 'Brits' but people from here, *irrespective* of their religious background.'

He just laughed: 'Give my head peace – you and your working-class unity.'

When I encountered Jim a few weeks later he met me with a wry smile.

'Mike, you should have put money on it. Not only were our best friends Northern Irish Catholics, they were Derry Republicans! There's no doubt that people from here have the same humour, the same easy-going nature... whereas, as you predicted, the other 'Brits' in the hotel were hard to communicate with.'

I shook my head in mock despair.

'Jim, on the one hand that type of comment makes me feel really hopeful, but on the other hand it really pisses me off – because so many people here can turn their antagonism on and off like a tap when it suits them. Yet despite all that we have in common, we're still slaughtering each other.'

• • •

Discussions with Loyalists, particularly with the UDA leadership, revealed to me much more of the tensions and contradictions which resided within the Protestant working class. Yes, within that community there existed the killers and the bigots, but there also existed humane people who fervently wanted to see a new society emerge, who were willing to reach an honourable accommodation with their Catholic neighbours. Yes, there were those whose politics were on the extreme Right, but there were also those with family traditions of long involvement in Belfast's Labour movement. There were the bewildered, the betrayed, the angry, the embittered, the dangerous and the reactionaries, as well as the idealists and the progressives – all were there, side by side.

The most paradoxical aspect was that not only were these internal tensions and contradictions mostly hidden from the general public, but even within the Protestant community they had never been fully aired or explored. This was partly a legacy of the violence which had forced many ordinary people to 'keep their heads down and their mouths shut', but also because there were no forums available to begin this exploration, no vehicles to carry forward any debate.

Andy Tyrie and I discussed ways of initiating such a debate, and the barriers we would encounter, not least the suspicion which would inevitably be engendered by any overtly political approach, especially at a time when the Protestant community felt itself increasingly under siege. Tyrie suggested taking the debate into working-class pubs and clubs in a less threatening, more entertaining, and hopefully more thought-provoking manner – by presenting these contradictions in a play. Could I help them accomplish this? he asked.

Out of this discussion the play *This is It!* was conceived (co-authored by myself, Andy Tyrie and Sammy Duddy), with Tyrie suggesting the plot – that of a young Protestant, who in 1981, convinced that his beloved Ulster is in a 'do or die' situation, decides to join the Rev Ian Paisley's 'Third Force'. This seemed an appropriate story-line, for the way the 'Big Man' was viewed within the Protestant working class reflected many of that community's internal contradictions. While some castigated him as a latter-day Grand Old Duke of York who had helped fill the prisons with young working-class Loyalists because of the way they had responded to his fiery rhetoric, many others viewed him with unquestioning respect. But for a few of the more farsighted he posed an obvious dilemma: could the very intransigence which so often proved to be a bulwark against Ulster's many enemies ultimately prove a barrier when the time came to move this society forward into a more pluralist, accommodating, and ultimately more secure, future?

As the play took shape we overindulged ourselves somewhat – adding poetry and songs and running the character list to ten. In retrospect this was to prove a major handicap when it came to having the play performed, for we soon discovered that there was a dearth of community drama groups within Belfast's Protestant working-class areas. Tyrie's solution was simple – if something of a surprise. He asked whether I could muster a cast from among my friends and associates in the Catholic community: 'Tell them I will guarantee their safety in Protestant areas.'

And so it was that, with willing offers of help from members of Ballymurphy People's Theatre, we almost managed to get a cast assembled. Equally important, the Ballymurphy recruits were fully supportive of the debate the play was intended to engender. However, the difficulties of trying to gather together a cast, arrange rehearsal times suitable for all, and a host of other logistical considerations – all new to us – proved impossible to surmount and it was never to see a live performance, either on the stage or before a pub audience.

The editors of *Theatre Ireland* had requested a copy of the play, and, considering it to be a progressive document and a purposeful use of drama, reprinted the complete text in their magazine. The BBC also got to hear of it and we were contacted to see if it could be rewritten as a radio play. The BBC interest, however, proved to be an unwelcome distraction. The producer who met with us made some surprising requests for the rewriting. Among other changes, he wanted a romantic relationship written in, to provide a 'love angle'. We refused and intensified the play's political message. Then, after almost a year of silence, he wrote saying that he hoped we were not disappointed that the play was being turned down, for the reasons he had "previously outlined" in his 'critique'. In fact, we had never received any such 'critique'; not that we minded this turn of events, for the changes he had suggested would only have commercialised the play and thwarted its grassroots purpose.

However, although the play was used for quite some time as a 'reading script' by numerous community groups, it eventually became just another document gathering dust on the shelves.[9]

•   •   •

All these community encounters – and in particular the rich diversity of ideas and opinions I was hearing on a daily basis, much of it at variance with the stereotypical analysis presented by the mass media – reawakened a long-felt determination to create a vehicle which would encourage as many people as possible to engage in exploration, debate and dialogue. One means was by getting people from both sides of the so-called 'divide' into direct face-to-face small-group discussions (something which has been attempted by different community activists throughout the Troubles). When Andy Tyrie left the UDA in March 1988, I had endeavoured to get him to join with individuals such as Father Wilson in a 'Cross-Community Think Tank', but although he and Des were willing, circumstances prevented the idea from coming to fruition. I also wanted to make my own contribution to creating a 'counter-information network', utilising booklets and other written material to stimulate and extend debate.

In 1993 these two elements – small-group discussions and accessible, informative booklets drawn from these discussions – were finally brought together when I initiated the 'Island Pamphlets' series. For the next five years output was sporadic, as I had to bear much of the costs myself (over a dozen prominent funding bodies having turned down requests for assistance), sustained by infrequent amounts of commercial desktop publishing and by Sheila's salary.

Then, in late 1998, funding was offered by both the EU Peace Programme

---

9   A revised version of this play is available as a free pdf file from mikeohall@hotmail.com

and the International Fund for Ireland, and with the support of the Farset Youth and Community Project, with whom I had had a long-standing association, the volume of work really took off. Between 1998 and 2005, operating as the Farset Community Think Tanks Project, I was able to facilitate a rich variety of discussion groups, embracing young people, senior citizens, victims, ex-prisoners, community workers, Loyalists, Republicans, those with disabilities, women's groups, community development practitioners, interface activists, cross-border workers... and many others. The geographical spread has been equally diverse: Think Tanks were convened on the Shankill, the Falls, Ardoyne, Glenbryn, Short Strand, Ballymacarrett and other parts of Belfast, as well as in Derry and Strabane. Initially people engaged in their own locally-based Think Tanks, but eventually, to my great satisfaction, community groups expressed the desire to cross the sectarian divide and engage in *joint* Think Tanks.

Furthermore, the funding allowed for 2000 copies of each pamphlet title to be distributed free of charge to over 100 community groups with whom I had built up working relationships during three decades of community activism. (To date, I have distributed over 150,000 pamphlets around the community network.)

The story of the Think Tanks Project – and its impact, at both an individual and a communal level – is described in more detail elsewhere[10], suffice to say that the pamphlet series is a world away from my first venture into pamphleteering. My 1973 document *Ireland: Dead or Alive?* was rhetoric-filled and imbued with the self-certainties of youth. In the Think Tank pamphlets, however, I strive to allow the participants to speak for themselves, and refrain from passing judgement. Assisting victims and the disempowered to have their voices heard came naturally to me, but back in 1973 I could never have imagined that I would also be sitting down with Loyalists, Republicans, Orangemen – and many others with whom I have fundamental disagreements – and assisting them to articulate and clarify their views for the benefit of the wider community. But I had come to realise that before this society can really move forward, we must all begin to listen to one another properly – and even *hear ourselves* properly – even if what is being said is unpalatable or hurtful. Only when all sections of this society feel that they are being accorded an equal input will we begin to find ways of reaching a lasting accommodation which will permit us to move into a more secure future.

The pamphlets have also had an impact further afield; indeed, some titles are currently being distributed by Israeli and Palestinian peace activists on both sides of their conflict interface. Such a development was no real surprise, as I have long believed that human beings of every nationality, colour and creed have identical needs, and humanity as a whole not only faces common problems but will hopefully find shared solutions to those problems. In the course of this sharing of experiences I have been brought into a working relationship with

---

10   A short history of Island Pamphlets was prepared for inclusion with a proposed CD-Rom containing the entire pamphlet series. It is available as a free pdf file from mikeohall@hotmail.com

some remarkable individuals from different arenas of conflict around the world. And some of those encounters have brought me back to my own beginnings: for example, through my association with Joe Camplisson's efforts to assist in the conflict between Moldova and its breakaway region of Transdniestria, I met Evgeni Berdnikov who, as a bewildered young tank commander, was part of the Warsaw Pact invasion of Czechoslovakia in 1968. The same event was a motivating force in both our lives, and all those years later we were to become associates in what are genuinely international efforts to find new ways of resolving violent conflict between peoples.[11]

● ● ●

On the day of the IRA ceasefire I was asked what it meant to me. I replied that, primarily, I felt deeply the horrendous waste of lives which had occurred, but I also felt that the Troubles had dissipated 30 years of my own energies. For although I had started out with a desire to promote fundamental socio-economic change and work towards new forms of participatory democracy, for over three decades I had found most of my energies largely sidetracked into trying to stop 'Prods and Taigs' from killing one another.

The Troubles will never be over for many people – they will bear its legacy the rest of their lives. Even I find that I can be 'ambushed by my emotions' (an apt description used by a friend of mind) at any time, any place. I can be sitting at a meeting, or driving in my car, and without warning a memory of one of the victims will flood back into my mind in all its original, painful intensity. And if this is how it can affect me, it is impossible to comprehend how it must still be affecting those who have directly lost loved ones.

And yet, I suppose my experience over the years has not been entirely negative. I have seen how generous and caring many people can be – from all communities – and how even hard-line individuals can reveal a genuine preparedness to work towards accommodation. Most importantly, I have repeatedly experienced at first hand just how willing many people are – from all backgrounds and aspirations – to enter into dialogue and debate, if provided with a conducive environment. I only hope that the Community Think Tanks Project, along with its complementary pamphlet series, has been able to play even a small part in encouraging and facilitating such debate and dialogue.

---

11 Camplisson, assisted by Barney McCaughey, Ian Bell, Lord Hylton and Yuri Ataman, has been involved in Moldova since 1992. A concise description of this initiative is to be found in Pamphlet No. 61, *The search for conflict resolution: lessons drawn from a community development strategy*. A much more in-depth account and analysis is to be found in the book *From Conflict Containment to Resolution*, by Joe Camplisson and myself, which I published in 2002 (£7.50 inclusive of postage in the UK; £9.00 elsewhere).